D1210257

*John Milton*

*Very Interesting* **VIP** *People*

*Bite-sized biographies of Britain's most
fascinating historical figures*

# *John Milton*

**VIP**
*Very Interesting People*

Gordon Campbell

**OXFORD**
UNIVERSITY PRESS

# OXFORD
## UNIVERSITY PRESS

Great Clarendon Street, Oxford ox2 6DP

Oxford University Press is a department of the University of Oxford.
It furthers the University's objective of excellence in research, scholarship,
and education by publishing worldwide in

Oxford New York

Auckland Cape Town Dar es Salaam Hong Kong Karachi
Kuala Lumpur Madrid Melbourne Mexico City Nairobi
New Delhi Shanghai Taipei Toronto

With offices in

Argentina Austria Brazil Chile Czech Republic France Greece
Guatemala Hungary Italy Japan Poland Portugal Singapore
South Korea Switzerland Thailand Turkey Ukraine Vietnam

Oxford is a registered trade mark of Oxford University Press
in the UK and in certain other countries

Published in the United States
by Oxford University Press Inc., New York

First published in the *Oxford Dictionary of National Biography* 2004
This paperback edition first published 2007

© Oxford University Press 2007

Database right Oxford University Press (maker)

First published 2007

British Library Cataloguing in Publication Data

Data available

Library of Congress Cataloging in Publication Data

Data available

Typeset by SPI Publisher Services, Pondicherry, India
Printed in Great Britain
on acid-free paper by
Ashford Colour Press Ltd, Gosport, Hampshire

ISBN 978–0–19–921761–8 (Pbk.)

10 9 8 7 6 5 4 3 2 1

# Contents

# *Preface*

The invitation to write the life of Milton for the *Oxford Dictionary of National Biography* came on a printed postcard. The founding editor, Colin Matthew, had scribbled a note on the corner: 'my Victorian predecessor thought this entry so important that he decided to write it himself. I have decided to entrust the task to you. The life of Milton will be one of the most important building blocks in our scholarly edifice'. I felt that I had been given a sacred charge, that of writing the authoritative account of the life of England's greatest poet, an account fit to stand alongside the lives of England's greatest dramatist (Peter Holland's Shakespeare) and England's greatest novelist (Rosemary Ashton's George Eliot), both of which have already been published in this series. Robert Faber, who as Project Director was the person who more than any other made the *Oxford DNB* happen, is a fine scholar-editor in the best traditions of Oxford University Press, and the formidable abilities that he brought to the task constituted a solid foundation on which I could rest my building block.

I was certainly in need of such a foundation, because I was uncertain about the shape of the block. The rough hewing was easy, in that the overall contours of Milton's life are familiar to scholars. Thereafter matters become difficult: contributors to the *Oxford DNB* must not use the opportunity to exercise their personal hobby horses, but sometimes the writer has to gamble on a hunch. New records of Milton's life are constantly being discovered, and each discovery makes a small impact on the overall shape of the life.

One example must suffice. Just as Milton's early poems are on one level studied as apprentice works that culminated in *Paradise Lost*, so scholars have scrutinized his early works with a view to discovering adumbrations of the future radical. One morning I met Jeremy Maule in Trinity College, Cambridge, and over coffee he gave me a present, which was a photocopy of some previously unknown records in the Hammersmith Record Office. The documents showed that on leaving Cambridge, Milton's place of worship became a Laudian chapel of ease at which his father was a churchwarden. This discovery raised the possibility that Milton was less radical in his youth than might have been imagined. At this point I had to write my *Oxford DNB* biography, and I had to be tentative, because this new evidence had no significant archival context. In the intervening years Edward Jones has discovered more than 50 new Milton documents from the 1620s and 1630s, and so has supplied the requisite context; were I writing afresh now, I could be more confident about my judgement of Milton in the early 1630s. In such ways the biography of an individual remains in a perpetual state of development, and the regular updatings of the

*Oxford DNB*'s online edition can accommodate fresh information and understandings. It is an edifice to which I am enormously proud to have contributed a building block.

*Gordon Campbell*

*January 2007*

## *About the author*

Gordon Campbell is Professor of Renaissance Studies at the University of Leicester. His recent work for OUP includes *The Oxford Dictionary of the Renaissance* (2003), *Renaissance Art and Architecture* (2004), and the Grove encyclopedias of Decorative Arts (2006), and Classical Art and Architecture (2007). His current projects (all with Thomas Corns) include a monograph on Milton's *De Doctrina Christiana* (2007), a new biography of Milton (2008), and the general editorship of a 12-volume edition of Milton's works, the first volumes of which will appear in 2008.

# Becoming a writer

1

*John Milton (1608–1674),* poet and polemicist, was born at 6.30 a.m. on Friday 9 December 1608 in the house at the sign of the Spread Eagle, Bread Street, London, and baptized in nearby All Hallows Church on 20 December, the third child of John Milton (1562–1647), and his wife, Sara, *née* Jeffrey (*c*.1572–1637). The house in Bread Street accommodated the scrivener's business of Milton's father, and was also the family home. The most remarkable feature of the domestic life of Milton's childhood was music: Milton's father was a composer, and the music that he wrote was designed for performance in private houses, without an audience. Milton grew up in a household in which music was performed, and his skills as a singer in consorts and as a player of the organ and the bass viol were acquired as a child in Bread Street.

## Education: St Paul's and Cambridge

Milton was initially educated at home by private tutors, including Thomas Young, a Scottish schoolmaster who eventually became master of Jesus College, Cambridge. In *Ad patrem* ('To my Father') Milton was later to express his gratitude that his father had paid for lessons in Latin, Greek, Hebrew, French, and Italian. It is likely that instruction in these languages began with private tutors; although Milton went on to study the ancient languages at school, modern languages were not taught in schools, and all of Milton's instruction in French and Italian (and possibly Spanish) was given by private tutors. At an unknown date between 1615 and 1621 Milton became a pupil at nearby St Paul's School; the most likely date is 1620, when the departure of Thomas Young for a pulpit in Hamburg may have prompted the decision to send Milton to school.

At St Paul's, Milton was taught by Alexander Gil the elder and became a friend of Alexander Gil the younger and of Charles Diodati. A lifetime later, Milton's widow told the antiquary John Aubrey that Milton was a poet at the age of ten. None of Milton's extant poems can be assigned to this date, but a few of his schoolboy juvenilia survive, including an imitation of Mantuan entitled *Apologus de rustico et hero* ('The Fable of a Peasant and his Master') and a Greek epigram, *Philosophus ad regem quendam* ('A philosopher to a certain king'). About 1874 a page (now at the University of Texas, Austin) apparently in Milton's youthful hand came to light, and it contains a prose theme on early rising and two Latin poems. Milton's earliest datable poems are English paraphrases of psalms 114 and 136; when Milton printed them in 1645 he said that they 'were done by the Author at fifteen years old', which was in 1624.

Early in 1625 Milton arrived in Cambridge, perhaps in time for the start of the Lent term on 13 January. On 12 February, on payment of 10*s*., he was admitted to Christ's College as a minor pensioner, a status below that of fellow-commoner but above that of sizar. The tutor to whom he was assigned was William Chappell, who was later to become provost of Trinity College, Dublin. On 9 April 1625 Milton presented himself to James Tabor, the university registrary, and formally matriculated at the university. Undergraduates did not necessarily return home during the university vacations, and it is likely that Milton stayed in college after term ended on 8 July, because a plague epidemic had broken out in London; when plague arrived in Cambridge at the beginning of August, Milton presumably left Cambridge to join his family at a retreat in the country. This outbreak of plague may be the 'slaughtering pestilence' to which Milton refers in his poem 'On the Death of a Fair Infant Dying of the Cough'; if so, the poem would seem to have been written in the winter of 1625–6. Alternatively, the subject of the poem may, as Edward Phillips recalled many years later, be Milton's niece (and Edward's sister) Anne, who died in January 1628, aged two.

Milton's earliest Latin poem from this period is a verse letter (later *Elegia prima*) addressed to his friend Charles Diodati, which seems to have been written from London early in April 1626, shortly before Milton returned to Cambridge. The deaths of four dignitaries in the autumn of 1626 offered occasions for Milton to venture into Latin memorial verse. Lancelot Andrewes, the distinguished scholar and divine, died on 25 September; Milton's commemorative poem (later *Elegia tertia*) for the celibate Andrewes ends with a startling adaptation of a line from Ovid (*Amores*, i.5) in which Ovid recalls an assignation with Corinna. On 26 September Richard Ridding, one of the university's esquire bedells, died, and Milton joined in the academic mourning with a memorial poem which he subsequently printed as *Elegia secunda*; 5 October brought the death of Nicholas Felton, who had succeeded Andrewes as bishop of Ely, and Milton once again used the occasion to compose a Latin poem. On 21 October Cambridge lost its vice-chancellor, John Gostlin, master of Gonville and Caius College and regius professor of medicine ('physic'), and once again Milton marked the occasion with a poem. It may have been in the same term that Milton turned his pen to vindictive anti-Catholic polemic in a series of Latin poems on the occasion of the Gunpowder Plot. Milton's contributions to the university celebrations of the defeat of the conspirators were the tiny verse-epic *In quintum Novembris* ('On the fifth of November'), four epigrams *In Proditionem Bombardicam* ('On the Gunpowder Plot'), and a fifth, *In inventorem bombardae* ('On the inventor of gunpowder'); the verse epic contains Milton's first portrayal of Satan.

The only remnants of Milton's prose to survive from this period are a Latin letter to Thomas Young and a collection of Latin academic exercises known as prolusions. The letter to Young was written on 26 March 1627; it was later printed as the first letter in Milton's *Epistolares familiares* ('Private letters'), but misdated as 26 March 1625. In this letter Milton alludes to a companion poem, which must be his verse letter to Young (later *Elegia quarta*). Six of Milton's seven Latin prolusions are speeches that he delivered to meet the academic requirements of the university and his college; four (1, 2, 3, and 7) are orations (*declamationes*) and two (4 and 5) are Milton's half of formal debates (*disputationes*). Prolusions 2, 3, and 5 were read in the 'Public Schools' (university lecture rooms, now known as 'Old Schools'), and prolusions 1, 4, and 7 were read in Christ's College. Prolusion 6 is not part of the statutory exercises, but is rather an address to Milton's fellow students at an entertainment (known as a 'salting') on the eve of the long vacation; this prolusion, which Milton delivered on or shortly before 4 July 1628, is preceded by a Latin oration addressed to his fellow students and followed by an English poem, 'On the Vacation Exercise'. This prolusion also contains the first reference to Milton's nickname, 'the Lady': just as the young Virgil *parthenias vulgo appellatus sit* ('was usually called the Lady'), so Milton became known as 'the Lady of Christ's'.

On 25 May and 11 June 1627 Milton was in London, where he signed two legal documents.

These absences from Cambridge during term time suggest that this may be the term when he fell out with William Chappell and was consequently sent down from the university. This period of suspension (or rustication) in London may have been the time when Milton wrote his mildly erotic *Elegia septima*, though it is possible that the poem was written as late as 1630. On returning to Cambridge, probably in the autumn of 1627, Milton was assigned to a new tutor, Nathaniel Tovey. When Milton's younger brother Christopher (1615–1693) was admitted to Christ's College in February 1631, he too was assigned to Tovey, which may imply that Milton had established a better relationship with Tovey than he had managed with Chappell.

Milton's final year as an undergraduate began badly when his friend Alexander Gil the younger was imprisoned for toasting the assassin of the duke of Buckingham, but Milton continued to study and occasionally to compose verse. He supplicated for his BA early in 1629 and later signed (apparently without scruple) the three articles of

religion in the university subscription book. The
spring of 1629 is the most likely date of composition for Milton's sonnet 'O nightingale' (later
Sonnet 1), his 'Song. On May Morning', and his
sensuous Latin poem *In adventum veris* ('On the
coming of spring'), later *Elegia quinta*.

## First religious and memorial works

The Cambridge MA is now taken without residence, but such was not the case in the seventeenth century, and Milton returned to Cambridge
in October 1629. It may have been during this
term that he wrote five Italian sonnets (later sonnets 2–6) and a *stanza di canzone*. The native-
speaker fluency of these youthful love poems is
an earnest of the formidable linguistic ability that
was later to be associated with Milton. One of
the sonnets is addressed to Diodati; another seems
furtively to address a lady called Emilia, who may
have been a member of the Italian protestant community in London or a product of Milton's enam-
oured imagination. Early on Christmas day 1629
Milton completed 'On the Morning of Christ's

Nativity'; shortly thereafter he sent a copy of the poem to Diodati, describing it in his accompanying Latin verse letter (later *Elegia sexta*) as a birthday gift to Christ, composed by the first light of dawn. In one of the introductory stanzas to the poem, Milton describes his 'hymn' as a 'humble ode', so aligning his Christian hymn with the pagan traditions of the ode; the poem is now known as the 'Nativity Ode'. It was Milton's first English poem on a religious theme, and he later indicated its importance in his spiritual and poetic development by placing it first in his 1645 and 1673 *Poems*. The 'Nativity Ode' inaugurated a triptych of poems based on the church calendar: Milton's unfinished poem in the metaphysical style, 'The Passion', was composed for Good Friday, probably in 1630, and 'Upon the Circumcision' marks new year's day, possibly in 1633.

In the autumn of 1630 the booksellers who had published the first folio of Shakespeare's plays began to make arrangements to produce a second folio, which was eventually published in 1632. For reasons that are not clear, Milton was asked

(or volunteered) to contribute a commendatory
poem; this was to be Milton's first published poem,
and he later collected it as 'On Shakespeare' and
dated it 1630. On new year's day 1631 Thomas
Hobson, the octogenarian driver of the Cambridge
to London coach, died in Cambridge, and university wits who had endured his reckless driving
were quick to mourn his passing. Milton joined
in the affectionate commemorations with two (or
possibly three) poems 'On the University Carrier';
the tone of the poems is light-hearted, but the
closing lines of the first poem, in which Death is
personified as the bedroom attendant in an inn,
constitute one of the most graceful descriptions
of mortality in English poetry. A more serious
memorial poem followed a few months later:
Jane Savage, the marchioness of Winchester, died
on 15 April 1631, and although Milton seems
not to have known her, he joined in the public
mourning with an 'Epitaph on the Marchioness
of Winchester', which he wrote on 'the banks of
Cam'.

# 'Fresh woods and pastures new'

2

## Hammersmith and Horton

Early in 1631 the Milton family moved to Hammersmith, which was then a hamlet in the parish of Fulham, some 6 miles west of London on the north bank of the Thames. Milton's father was certainly in residence in April 1631, when he was assessed for poor relief. Two months later, on 7 June 1631, a newly established chapel of ease was consecrated by Bishop Laud; Milton's father became a churchwarden, and, on coming down from Cambridge, Milton became a parishioner. He had sworn on supplicating for his MA to continue his studies for an additional five years; two years later (in 1639) he would have been eligible to apply for the degree of bachelor of divinity (Latin *sanctae theologiae baccalaureus*). This oath was merely the vestige of an earlier custom, but Milton seems to have taken it seriously, because he chose to spend the next five years in private study; he was later to claim that he was making good the deficiencies of his Cambridge education. In signing the subscription book to take his MA, Milton once again acknowledged the liturgy and doctrine of the Church of England and the supremacy of the king; he was eventually to ignore the liturgy, repudiate several key aspects of the doctrine, and applaud the execution of the king to whom he had sworn allegiance.

From time to time Milton interrupted his private studies in order to compose verse, but there is no evidence for the dates of several important works that seem to be products of the early 1630s. The Latin poem addressed to his father, *Ad patrem*, may be a product of this period, as may Milton's English translation of Horace's fifth ode, *Ad Pyrrham*. His pastoral entertainment, *Arcades*, was performed in the garden of Harefield, the estate of the dowager countess of

Derby near Uxbridge. The poised and sprightly
twin poems 'L'Allegro' and 'Il Penseroso' may date
from this period, if indeed they were written at
the same time, but the countryside described in
'L'Allegro' contains no features that enable it to
be tied to a specific place and time. Similarly,
'At a Solemn Music' and 'On Time' are likely to
have been written during this period, but cannot
be dated with any precision. His sonnet 'How
soon hath time' (later Sonnet 7), however, can be
assigned with some confidence to December 1632,
close to Milton's twenty-fourth birthday.

In 1634 Milton was asked to compose the text of
a masque which was to be mounted in Ludlow
in honour of the inauguration of John Egerton,
earl of Bridgewater, as lord president of Wales;
Ludlow is in England rather than Wales, but it
is in the Welsh marches and was the seat of the
court of marches, over which the earl of Bridgewater was to preside. The music for the masque
was written by Henry Lawes, who had probably commissioned Milton to compose the text.
The masque was performed at Ludlow Castle on

Monday 29 September 1634. Three of the earl's children (all of whom had acted before) played the central roles, and Henry Lawes acted the part of the Attendant Spirit. The idea that Milton travelled to Ludlow and acted the part of Comus is a scholarly fantasy without foundation. In 1637 or early in 1638 Lawes published Milton's text (without any indication of its authorship) as *A Maske Presented at Ludlow Castle*, and Milton reprinted it in his *Poems* of 1645. Since the late seventeenth century the masque has been known as *Comus*; to call the masque after the tempter is rather like referring to *Paradise Lost* as *Satan*, but the title is now firmly established. Later in the year, Alexander Gil wrote a Latin epithalamium, and sent a copy to Milton; on 4 December Milton replied, enclosing a recently composed translation of Psalm 114 into Greek verse.

On 12 May 1636 Milton's father resigned as assistant to the Company of Scriveners on the grounds of his 'removal to inhabit in the country'. This phrase (in a manuscript that is now lost) indicates the retirement of Milton's family to Horton,

Buckinghamshire (later Berkshire). Milton may have used the nearby libraries at Eton College and Langley (the Kedermister Library) to support his programme of private study, because London was much less accessible than it had been in Hammersmith. It was about this time that Milton started to record titbits from his voluminous reading in a commonplace book (now in the British Library), which he continued to use until after the Restoration.

## 'Lycidas'

Less than a year after Milton had settled with his parents into the rural seclusion of Horton, his mother, Sara, died, on 3 April 1637. Milton and his father buried her in the aisle of the chancel of Horton church; the inscribed blue stone still bears her name. Milton seems not to have written a poem in her memory, but soon occasion arose for him to write his greatest memorial poem, one that is arguably the finest short poem in the English language. The occasion of 'Lycidas' was the death of Edward King, a fellow of Christ's College who had drowned off the coast of Anglesey on 10 August 1637. King had been a younger contemporary of Milton at Christ's College, and had been awarded a fellowship by royal mandate. The myth that Milton was aggrieved because he had been robbed of the fellowship for which he was destined was invented in the eighteenth century, and is based on the groundless assumption that an academic post, with its attendant obligations of celibacy and ordination in the Church of England, would have been the highest calling to which Milton might have aspired. In fact Milton was contemptuous of Cambridge, and in any case he was ineligible for election, because the statutes of the college prohibited the election of more than one fellow from any county; the future dean of Lincoln Michael Honywood was, like Milton, a native of London, and so Milton could not have been elected to a fellowship as long as Honywood was in post.

The death of the poet and playwright Ben Jonson on 16 August, six days after the death of Edward King, was marked in Oxford by a collection of memorial poems entitled *Jonsonus virbius*. It is possible that this volume provided a stimulus for the poets of Cambridge to assemble a rival volume in memory of King, who had lacked Jonson's great gifts as a poet, but had none the less published ten competent Latin poems. Milton was asked to contribute a poem, and in November 1637 copied a draft of 'Lycidas' into his poetical notebook (now in Trinity College, Cambridge, and so known as the Trinity manuscript). The poem was published in *Justa Edouardo King naufrago ab amicis moerentibus, amoris et mneias charin* ('Obsequies to Edward King, drowned by shipwreck, in token of love and remembrance, by his grieving friends') late in 1638. Milton had chosen to write in English, and his poem was placed at the end of the English section of the volume, which had a separate title-page (*Obsequies to the Memory of Mr Edward King*). Most of the poems in the volume were written in the fashionable idiom of the metaphysical poem, often in imitation of John Donne. Milton chose to ignore this contemporary enthusiasm for wittily expressed grief in favour of the traditional genre of the pastoral elegy.

His poem originated in a desire to commemorate King, but in the act of composition Milton transcended his ostensible subject and produced a meditation on human mortality that retains the power to move readers centuries after the death of King and those who mourned him.

The origins of Milton's disenchantment with the Caroline church are not clear, but the earliest unambiguous evidence would seem to be enshrined in 'Lycidas', in which the apostle Peter censures the English church. Satire directed against the church had been a part of pastoral elegy since Petrarch, and Milton took advantage of this convention to mount an attack on the greed of the clergy, whom he stigmatizes as 'blind mouths'; he does, however, furnish Peter with a bishop's mitre, because in 1637 Milton was still content with the notion that it was Peter who had inaugurated the succession of bishops.

'Lycidas' concludes with an affirmation that when grieving has finished, life must go on: 'Tomorrow to fresh woods and pastures new'. Milton had grieved privately for his mother and publicly for Edward King, and he then turned to his plans to travel to the woods and pastures of Italy. He sought advice from Sir Henry Wotton, who had retired from his diplomatic career to become provost of Eton, which was within a few miles of Horton. On 6 April 1638 Milton wrote to Wotton, enclosing a copy of *Comus* and mentioning his intention to travel to Italy in the next few weeks. Wotton's reply, which Milton printed in the edition of *Comus* in his 1645 *Poems*, contained advice about the best route and about deportment, together with an introduction to the English ambassador in Paris.

## Travels in Italy, 1638–1639

In May 1638 Milton left England for a tour of the continent that was to last approximately fifteen months. He first travelled from London to Paris, where he met the ambassador of King Charles, Viscount Scudamore of Sligo. Lord Scudamore arranged for Milton to meet Hugo Grotius, the learned Dutch jurist who was living in Paris as the ambassador of Queen Kristina of Sweden.

On leaving Paris, Milton travelled south to Nice, along the coast to Genoa, thence to Leghorn by ship, and then inland via Pisa to Florence, where he arrived in June 1638 for a visit of about five months. During this first visit to Florence, Milton participated in the meetings of at least two Florentine academies (the Svogliati and the Apatisti) and so became acquainted with the learned men of the city, several of whom composed tributes to Milton which he was later to print in his 1645 *Poemata*.

Milton's attendance at the weekly meetings of the Svogliati in the new *palazzo* of the Gaddi family (later the Hotel Astoria) enabled him to meet the poet Antonio Malatesti, who subsequently dedicated *La Tina*, an erotic sonnet sequence, 'al grande poeta inghilese Giovanni Milton Londra' ('to the great English poet John Milton of London'). At these meetings Milton also met the scholar Benedetto Buonmattei, to whom Milton subsequently wrote proposing additions to his *Della lingua Toscana* (the suggestions were ignored) and Vincenzo Galilei, the illegitimate son of Galileo. It may have been Vincenzo who arranged for Milton to visit Galileo, either in the astronomer's house at Arcetri or in Vincenzo's house on the Costa San Giorgio, where Galileo was staying for medical treatment; Milton was later to recall the visit in *Areopagitica* (1644). On 6/16 September 1638 (i.e. 6 September in England's Julian calendar and 16 September in Italy's Gregorian calendar) Milton read one of his own Latin poems to the academicians, who judged it to be 'molto erudita'. There is a late tradition to the effect that Milton visited Vallombrosa while staying in Florence, but there is no evidence and little likelihood that such a visit took place; Milton's allusion to the 'autumnal leaves that strew the brook / In Vallombrosa' (*Paradise Lost*, book 1, ll. 302–3) derives from Ariosto, not from a recollection of an excursion to the monastery at Vallombrosa.

In October 1638 Milton travelled south to Siena and thence to Rome, where he stayed for about two months. On 20/30 October he dined in the English College, where the pilgrim book records the presence of Milton and his unnamed servant as well as three other English guests. In December Milton journeyed on to Naples in the company of an unidentified traveller whom Milton later described as a hermit; he was presumably a Carmelite friar. This well-connected hermit introduced Milton to his Neapolitan host, Giovanni Battista Manso, marchese di Villa, to whom Milton later addressed *Mansus*, a poem that sought to demonstrate in its elegant Latin hexameters that Manso, who had been the patron of Torquato Tasso and Giambattista Marino, had once again offered hospitality to a poet. Milton had originally planned to go on from Naples to Sicily and Greece, but he decided to abandon these plans and travel slowly home; he later attributed this decision (in the *Defensio secunda*) to 'the sad tidings of civil war from England ... For I thought it base that I should travel abroad at my ease for the cultivation of my mind while my fellow citizens at home were fighting for liberty'.

In January 1639 Milton returned to Rome, where he met (or renewed his acquaintance with) the poet Giovanni Salzilli (to whom he later addressed his Latin poem *Ad Salsillam*), the German scholar and Catholic convert Lukas Holste, and Cardinal Francesco Barberini. Holste, who was secretary and librarian to Cardinal Barberini, showed Milton around the Barberini Library and presented him with a copy of his recently published bilingual edition of the axioms of the later Pythagoreans; on learning that Milton was returning to Florence, Holste asked him to visit the Laurentian Library to copy parts of a Medicean codex for him. During this visit to Rome, Milton attended at least two musical events. He was present at a recital given by the singer Leonora Baroni and subsequently wrote three conventionally enraptured epigrams in her honour, *Ad Leonoram Romae canentem* ('To Leonora, Singing in Rome'). On 17/27 February he attended a comic opera (Rospigliosi's *Chi soffre, speri*) mounted by Cardinal Francesco Barberini in the vast theatre of the newly completed Palazzo Barberini; the audience of 3500 included Cardinal Mazarin. Milton later recalled that he was greeted at the door by Cardinal Barberini, who granted him a private audience the next day; Barberini was prime minister of Rome and chief adviser to his uncle Pope Urban VIII, but he was also protector of the English, and in that capacity regularly offered hospitality and assistance to travellers such as Milton.

In March 1639 Milton returned to Florence, where he tried unsuccessfully to obtain permission to copy the manuscript for Holste. He again attended the Thursday meetings of the Svogliati, reading his Latin poems on 7/17 and 14/24 March. In April Milton travelled to Bologna and Ferrara and thence to Venice, where he stayed for at least a month. He shipped home the collection of books that he had amassed in his travels, including at least one case of music books containing works by Claudio Monteverdi (who was still living in Venice), Luca Marenzio, Orazio Vecchi, and Don Carlo Gesualdo. He then proceeded from Venice to Verona and Milan, through Lombardy and the Apennine Alps to Lake Geneva and on to Geneva, where he visited the theologian Giovanni (or Jean) Diodati, uncle of his friend Charles Diodati; if he had not heard the news of Charles's death earlier, Milton may have been told in Geneva. In July he returned to England through France, and shortly thereafter published a Latin poem in memory of Diodati; the only known copy of this edition of the *Epitaphium Damonis* ('Epitaph for Damon'), the greatest of Milton's Latin poems, survives in the British Library.

# Polemicist and teacher

## 3

## Critic of the church

On returning to London, Milton took lodgings at the house of a tailor called Russell in St Bride's Churchyard (near Fleet Street), where he inaugurated his career as a schoolmaster by assuming responsibility for the education of his nephews Edward and John Phillips. He soon moved to a large house in Aldersgate Street, where he was able to take on additional pupils. Milton's life in the 1640s was divided between his duties as a teacher and his avocation as a polemicist involved in the controversy about church government and initiating a debate about divorce.

In 'Lycidas', Milton's attack on the Caroline church had centred on what he saw as ecclesiastical cupidity; when he renewed his attack four years later his censure was directed towards episcopacy, the system whereby churches are governed by bishops. Episcopacy had been enshrined in the Elizabethan settlement, but throughout the late sixteenth and early seventeenth centuries, vigorous opposition had been voiced by reformers who felt that episcopacy was a vestige of Roman Catholicism and an impediment to the realization of a full reformation. Under Elizabeth the crown had assumed the title of 'supreme governor' of the English church, and so the monarch stood at the head of the episcopate. The crown became associated with the episcopal cause, and so it seems likely that Milton's anti-monarchical sentiments of the 1650s had their origins in his anti-episcopal stance of the early 1640s.

The debate about episcopacy had rumbled on for decades, but in 1637 had erupted because of the indictment of three prominent puritans (Henry Burton, John Bastwick, and William Prynne) for publishing tracts which attacked episcopacy; the court of Star Chamber sentenced the three defendants to torture and mutilation on the scaffold and subsequent incarceration. By 1641 the combatants in the debate had begun to write polemical treatises: Joseph Hall, bishop of Norwich, had published a defence of episcopacy called *An Humble Remonstrance to the High Court of Parliament*, and a few months later, in March 1641, a group of puritan ministers known collectively by their initials as Smectymnuus (Stephen Marshall, Edward Calamy, Milton's former tutor Thomas Young, Matthew Newcomen, and William Spurstow), responded to Hall with *An Answer to a Book Entitled 'An Humble Remonstrance'*. In April Hall hit back with *A Defence of the Humble Remonstrance*, to which Smectymnuus replied in June with *A Vindication of the Answer of the Humble Remonstrance*; the following month Hall responded yet again with his *Short Answer to the Tedious Vindication of Smectymnuus*.

## Making of an Independent

At this point Milton entered the lists with the first of his five anti-prelatical pamphlets, *Of reformation touching church discipline in England and the causes that hitherto have hindered it*, which was published between 12 and 31 May 1641. This anonymous tract outlines the pernicious effects of episcopacy, but sets aside the theoretical arguments about church government in favour of fulminations against the episcopate which culminate in a call for the execution of bishops and a prophecy that they will spend eternity being tortured in hell. In the same month that Milton's first tract was published, the patristic scholar James Ussher, archbishop of Armagh, published *The Judgement of Dr Rainolds Touching the Original of Episcopacy*, in which he sought to confirm the views of the Elizabethan churchman John Rainolds by recourse to patristic authority. Milton responded with *Of prelatical episcopacy, and whether it may be deduced from the apostolical times by virtue of those testimonies which are alleged to that purpose in some late treatises, one whereof goes under the name of James, archbishop of Armagh.* In this short tract Milton contended that to support episcopacy by resort to the church fathers was tantamount to denying the sufficiency of scripture, and also lent hostages to fortune in providing arguments that could be used to defend Roman Catholicism; throughout the tract Milton maintains a civil tone with his learned opponent, but he none the less declares Ussher's scholarship to be wanting in several important particulars.

Milton's third anti-prelatical tract was a response to Hall's *Defence of the Humble Remonstrance*, which had been published in April 1641; Milton replied in July with *Animadversions upon the Remonstrant's Defence Against Smectymnuus*. The qualified deference that Milton had shown to Archbishop Ussher is nowhere in evidence; instead Milton mounts an excoriating personal attack on Bishop Hall. He returns to the attack on the greed of the clergy first articulated in 'Lycidas'; the reticence of pastoral elegy has given way to the savagery of seventeenth-century polemic, and Milton pours vitriol on those who would use the church to amass personal fortunes.

In 1641 episcopalian apologists assembled a tract (possibly edited by Archbishop Ussher) entitled

*Certain brief treatises written by learned men concerning the ancient and modern government of the church.* At the end of January 1642 Milton published his reply, *The Reason of Church Government Urged Against Prelaty*; the title-page (which is dated 1641) reveals the identity of this tireless polemicist as 'Mr John Milton'. The decision to shed the cloak of anonymity is reflected in the body of the tract by the emergence of a newly radical Milton who is willing to 'divulge unusual things of myself' in an autobiographical digression. Whereas in *Of Prelatical Episcopacy* and *Animadversions* Milton had argued as a presbyterian within the national church of England, in *The Reason of Church Government* he moves away from state presbyterianism towards independent congregationalism, which had taken root in the puritan colonies of America and had been re-exported to England as radical tolerationism: Milton had not become a sectarian, but he now differed from the presbyterians in arguing for a measure of toleration, so adumbrating the explicitly tolerationist position that he was to take up in his later years.

Milton's fifth and final anti-prelatical tract, published in April 1642, is entitled *An apology against a pamphlet called 'A modest confutation of a scandalous and scurrilous libel entitled Animadversions'*. The anonymous *Modest Confutation* to which Milton replies had been published the previous month; its authorship is uncertain, but it may be the joint work of Joseph Hall and his son Robert. The attack that Milton had directed against Bishop Hall in *Animadversions* is heartily reciprocated in the *Modest Confutation*, which accuses Milton of personal immorality. Milton was always sensitive to personal attacks, and although this sensitivity did not inhibit him in the return of fire in these polemical skirmishes, he always insisted on defending his personal purity: on this occasion he testily insisted that he had never visited brothels as an undergraduate, but that he had observed the irresponsible behaviour of fellow undergraduates who were in due course to rise to senior positions in the church while never managing to shed their adolescent irresponsibility. In the course of the five years between late-1637 and mid-1642 Milton had moved from being a constructively critical member of the national church to taking up the cause of ecclesiastical reform, and eventually becoming an impassioned opponent of ecclesiastical abuses: he had become an Independent.

## Marriage, separation, and writings on divorce

In June 1642 Milton embarked on a journey to Forest Hill, in Oxfordshire, with a view to collecting an interest payment of £12 from Richard Powell, an improvident landowner and magistrate to whom Milton's father had lent £300 in 1627. Edward Phillips was later to record that 'after a month's stay, home he returns a married man, that went out a bachelor, his wife being Mary the eldest daughter of Mr Richard Powell'. After the wedding Milton took his seventeen-year-old bride home to his house on Aldersgate Street. A few weeks later Mary returned to her parental home. The initial extension of what was intended as a short separation may have been occasioned by the outbreak of civil war on 22 August, when King

Charles raised his standard at Nottingham, but it eventually became clear that the newly wedded couple were estranged.

The reasons for the almost instantaneous collapse of Milton's marriage are not known, but the seriousness of the rift is attested by the fact that Milton redirected his scholarly energies from episcopacy to divorce. In seventeenth-century England a divorce that permitted remarriage could be granted only by parliament; ordinary citizens without access to parliament had to turn to the ecclesiastical courts, which had the power only to grant a form of judicial separation called divorce *a mensa et thoro* ('from table and bed'). For centuries canon law had stipulated six grounds for divorce: sexual offences (adultery, sodomy, and bestiality), impotence, physical cruelty, infidelity (that is, apostasy), entry into holy orders, and consanguinity; Milton's wife may have deserted him, but in England desertion did not constitute grounds for divorce until 1857. On 1 August 1643 Milton published *The doctrine and discipline of divorce, restored to the good of both sexes from the bondage of canon law and other mistakes to Christian freedom*, in which he argued that the traditional grounds for divorce were insufficient, and that a man should be able to divorce his wife if the marriage had become spiritually and emotionally barren. Milton does not argue for equal rights for the woman in marriage, but his views none the less anticipate in several respects the position that English law reached in 1977, when it was decreed that the sole ground for divorce was the irretrievable breakdown of a marriage.

On 2 February 1644 Milton published a heavily revised second edition of *Doctrine and Discipline of Divorce* which he addressed to the English parliament and the Westminster Assembly; the reason for the twofold audience was that if the assembly approved of Milton's suggestions, parliament would probably have enshrined new divorce rules in law.

Milton's practical experience of a domestic classroom had led him to reflect on the education appropriate to young members of the governing class. The educational reformer Samuel Hartlib asked Milton to set out his views on the education of children. Milton replied with *Of Education*, a public letter to Hartlib which was published on 5 June 1644. The pamphlet sets out the daunting programme of a Miltonic education, which encompasses ancient languages (Latin, Greek, Hebrew, Aramaic, Syriac) and a huge range of academic and practical subjects; the only modern language mentioned is Italian, which Milton magisterially claims can be 'easily learned at any odd hour'. The boys in this academy would be prepared to govern a nation, but also to fight for it and oversee its agriculture. To teach in such an academy would not, Milton concedes, be a task for anyone 'that counts himself a teacher, but will require sinews almost equal to those which Homer gave Ulysses'. Milton's educational aspirations were heroic, but his practical efforts as a teacher failed to produce highly educated warrior princes: the Miltonic education of his two nephews equipped them for only the modest profession of hack writing.

On 6 August 1644 Milton published his second divorce tract, again addressed to parliament; this tract is a translation and condensation of chapters 15 to 47 of the second book of *De regno Christi* ('On the kingdom of Christ') by Martin Butzer (or Bucer), which Milton called *The Judgement of Martin Bucer Concerning Divorce*. A week later, on 13 August, Herbert Palmer condemned Milton's divorce tracts in a sermon to parliament, and eleven days later parliament was asked by the Company of Stationers to control unlicensed and unregistered books, including Milton's *Doctrine and Discipline of Divorce*.

## Reconciliation and return to divorce

This attempt to stifle Milton's tract may have been the spark that ignited his wrath against those who would censor books before publication. *Areopagitica* was Milton's belated response to the licensing order of June 1643, which stipulated that all books had to be examined by a censor prior to publication. His tract, published on 23 November 1644, takes the form of an oration addressed to parliament, which Milton accused of reviving the oppressive measures of a Star Chamber decree of July 1637. Milton's Greek title proposes an analogy between the English parliament and the ancient council of Athens which met on the Areopagus (the 'Hill of Ares' north-west of the Acropolis), and also recalls the *Areopagiticus*, an oration by the ancient orator Isocrates. In the short term Milton was unsuccessful, because parliament ignored his plea; in subsequent centuries, however, *Areopagitica* came to be valued as the most eloquent defence in English of the right to publish without prior censorship. It has also been invoked as a defence of free speech, but in fact the limits of Miltonic toleration were strictly circumscribed, and include a denial of the rights of Roman Catholics to publish works in defence of their religion.

On 4 March 1645 Milton published his third and fourth divorce tracts, *Tetrachordon* and *Colasterion*. Both titles are taken from ancient Greek. *Tetrachordon* is an adjective meaning 'four-stringed', and the neuter suffix links it to the word for musical instrument; Milton is straining to suggest that in the tract he is harmonizing the four main biblical treatments of marriage and divorce. *Colasterion* is a noun which refers to a place or instrument of torture; Edward Phillips translated the term as 'rod of correction', which may imply that he understood his uncle to be alluding to the beating that he had inflicted on his opponent, who in this instance was the anonymous author of *An Answer to a Book Entitled 'The Doctrine and Discipline of Divorce'*, which had been published on 19 November 1644.

Milton's reputation as an advocate of divorce had incurred the obloquy of the ecclesiastical establishment, but at least one person seems to have invoked Milton to justify an otherwise unsanctioned divorce: Mrs Attaway, the lace-woman turned radical preacher, spoke approvingly of Milton's tract, and deserted her ungodly husband for William Jenny, the godly husband of another woman. It was about this time that news reached the Powell family to the effect that Milton was planning to divorce Mary and marry the

daughter of one Dr Davies. Phillips reports that
this prospect 'caused them to set all engines on
work to restore the late married woman' (Masson,
3.437); a reconciliation was effected, probably in
mid-1645, and when Milton moved into a large
house in Barbican in the autumn of 1645, he was
joined by Mary. Their daughter Anne was born
on 7 July 1646; Milton entered the details on the
flyleaf of his family Bible (now in the British
Library), where he had recently begun to record
his family's births and deaths.

Milton's father died in March 1647, and that
autumn Milton moved with his young family to a
smaller house in High Holborn, backing onto Lincoln's Inn Fields. In the following year, on 25 October, his daughter Mary was born. The move to
a smaller house may reflect a diminution of (or
even a conclusion to) Milton's career as a teacher.
In this period of relative calm between the end of
teaching and the onset of his career as a public servant, Milton turned to private study and writing.
It may have been in 1648 that he wrote his *Brief
History of Moscovia*, published posthumously in

1683. At the same time it seems likely that Milton was gathering materials for his *History of Britain*, the first four books of which he drafted, according to his own account, in the six weeks between the execution of the king on 30 January 1649 and his own appointment as Latin secretary on 13 March.

## Poetry, 1641–1648

The poems that Milton wrote in the 1640s were all short occasional pieces, and for the most part consisted of sonnets. After the battle of Edgehill on 23 October 1642, the army of Charles I advanced towards London, causing widespread panic in the capital. Milton's 'Captain or Colonel' (later Sonnet 8), which is entitled 'When the assault was intended to the City' in the Trinity manuscript, may have been occasioned by the prospect of the fall of London. The next poem in the Trinity manuscript is 'Lady, that in the prime of earliest youth' (later Sonnet 9), which uses the parable of the wise and foolish virgins to praise an unidentified lady. This poem may have been followed by 'To the Lady Margaret Ley' (later Sonnet 10).

Lady Margaret was the daughter of James Ley, the first earl of Marlborough, and the second wife of Captain John Hobson, who had fought on the side of parliament; the Hobsons lived near Milton on Aldersgate Street, and Milton was a regular visitor to their home during the years when he was separated from Mary.

In 1645 Milton decided to collect his youthful poems. The edition was published as *Poems of Mr John Milton, both English and Latin*; the edition is dated 1645, but may have been published on 2 January 1646, which is the date that George Thomason inscribed on his copy, which is now in the British Library. The English section was a miscellany consisting of early poems and translations, Milton's first ten sonnets (including the Italian sonnets), and *Comus*, which Milton had revised since its last publication. The Latin section (which included a few Greek poems) had a separate title-page, *Joannis Miltoni Londoniensis poemata. Quorum pleraque intra annum aetatis vigesimum conscripsit* ('Poems by John Milton of London, most of which were Written before he was Twenty'); this section was paginated separately, and was divided into a book of poems in elegiac couplets (*Elegiarum liber*) and a collection of poems in various metres (*Sylvarum liber*). The publisher, Humphrey Moseley, commissioned a portrait of Milton from the engraver William Marshall. The portrait is unflattering, and when Milton was shown it, he sought a cruel revenge by composing a few lines of Greek verse, which the hapless (and Greekless) Marshall engraved beneath the portrait; the verses invite the reader to laugh at the portrait, which Milton says is not a picture of him but of the incompetence of the engraver. It seems possible that the cruel humour of the God of *Paradise Lost* has its origins in the personality of his creator.

Milton felt that his *Tetrachordon* had been ignored, and lamented this injustice in 'A book was writ of late called *Tetrachordon*' (later Sonnet 11), the precise date of which is unknown: it seems to have been written too late for inclusion in the 1645 *Poems*, and its position in the Trinity manuscript may imply a date of composition in 1647.

This sense of injured merit is extended to all four of Milton's divorce tracts in 'On the Detraction which Followed upon my Writing Certain Treatises' (later Sonnet 12); again the date of composition is uncertain, but the winter of 1645–6 is not unlikely, and so the numbering of sonnets 11 and 12 is normally reversed in modern editions. The sonnet in praise of the music of Henry Lawes ('To Mr Henry Lawes, on his Airs', later Sonnet 13) can be dated more precisely, because the first of the three drafts in the Trinity manuscript is dated 9 February '1645' (which would now be called 1646: according to the Julian calendar, the new year started on 25 March). In 1646 or early 1647 Milton wrote a twenty-line poem 'On the new forcers of conscience under the Long Parliament', which concludes with the etymological epigram 'new *Presbyter* is but old *Priest* writ large'.

On 16 December 1646 Katharine Thomason, the wife of Milton's friend George Thomason, was buried in the south aisle of St Dunstan-in-the-West; shortly thereafter Milton wrote a sonnet in her memory (later Sonnet 14). A few weeks later, on 23 January 1647, he returned to Latin poetry with an ode to John Rouse, librarian of the Bodleian, Oxford, to accompany a presentation copy of his 1645 *Poems* intended to replace a copy that had gone astray. In April 1648, on the eve of the second civil war, Milton translated psalms 80–88 from the Hebrew. His next poem is a direct reaction to one event in that war: General Lord Fairfax besieged Colchester on 14 June, and the town fell on 27 August; during the siege Milton wrote a sonnet in praise of Fairfax (later Sonnet 15). By the end of the year the Rump Parliament had decided to indict the king, which set England on a course that was to carry Milton into a public role as a writer and translator in the service of the English republic.

# Champion of the republic

4

## Secretary for foreign tongues

Between 15 and 29 January 1649, during the trial of Charles I, Milton wrote his *Tenure of Kings and Magistrates*, which argued on its title-page that 'it is lawful ... for any who have the power, to call to account a Tyrant or wicked King and after due conviction, to depose, and put him to death'. Charles was executed on 30 January 1649, and a fortnight later, on 13 February, Milton's tract was published. At noon on 13 March the council of state decided to invite Milton to be secretary for foreign tongues. He was appointed two days later, on Thursday 15 February, at an annual salary of £288 13*s*. 6½*d*. Before he could take up his post on the following Tuesday, parliament abolished the

House of Lords (17 February) and the monarchy (19 February), so Milton entered the service of a nascent republic. The post included accommodation in Whitehall, but as an interim measure Milton lodged next to the Bull-head tavern in Charing Cross, opening on to Spring Garden. In November Milton moved with his household into an apartment formerly occupied by Sir John Hippesley at the Scotland Yard end of Whitehall; when the art collection of Charles I was put on sale in nearby Somerset House, Milton was given a warrant (dated 18 June 1650) to choose some hangings from the royal collection 'for the furnishing of his lodging in Whitehall'.

In the first instance Milton's duties in the service of the council of state consisted for the most part in translating international correspondence into the Latin of diplomacy; this was a task which he discharged throughout his period as a civil servant, but he quickly assumed more important tasks alongside these routine duties. On 28 March the council ordered:

that Mr. Milton be appointed to make some observations upon the complication of interests which is now amongst the several designers against the peace of the Commonwealth; And that it be ready to be printed with the Papers out of Ireland which the House hath ordered to be printed. (Masson, 4.87)

The *Articles of Peace* were published on 16 May, and Milton's *Observations* were printed as an appendix. From Milton's English perspective the native Irish were barbarians who massacred civilized English settlers and soldiers. The anachronistic condemnation of Milton's hostile attitude does not facilitate historical understanding, but it is undeniably the case that the consequences of such hostility were immediately felt in the massacres by Cromwell's forces at Drogheda and Wexford, and still reverberate in Anglo-Irish politics.

On 9 February 1649, ten days after the execution of King Charles, *Eikōn Basilikē* had been published; the Greek title means 'image of the king'. This book, which purported to have been written by the king (and was in fact written by his chaplain John Gauden), achieved an instant popularity, and within a year had been published in some fifty editions in various languages. The council of state was concerned that sympathy for the king could subvert the Commonwealth, and so commissioned an official reply. Initially John Selden had been asked to respond, but when he declined the council turned to Milton. In October Milton published his reply, which he entitled *Eikonoklastēs*; the literal meaning of the Greek title is 'imagebreaker', but the term was meant to evoke the surname adopted by Greek emperors 'who in their zeal to the command of God, after long tradition of idolatry in the church, took courage and broke all superstitious images to pieces'.

## Milton's three defences

The regicide had alarmed continental Europe, and one of the first scholarly defences of Charles I, the *Defensio regia pro Carolo I* ('The royal defence of Charles I') written by the learned French protestant Claude de Saumaise (Claudius

Salmasius), reached England in May 1649. On
8 January 1650 the council of state ordered
Milton to prepare a reply to this damaging
book, which threatened to delay the resumption
of normal trade relations with the continent.
Milton's reply, *Joannis Miltonii Angli defensio pro
populo Anglicano contra Claudii Anonymi, aliàs
Salmasii, defensionem regiam* ('The defence of
John Milton, Englishman, on behalf of the people
of England against the royal defence of Claudius
the Anonymous, otherwise Salmasius') was not
published until 24 February 1651; it is now known
by the non-Miltonic title *Defensio prima* or *First
Defence*. In the text Milton excuses his delay on
grounds both of a lack of time to write and of
insufficient health for the labour of writing; even
now, he explains in his preface, his health is so
poor and precarious that he has to take a break
virtually every hour. Among the purchasers of this
volume was the second earl of Bridgewater, who
as a child had acted the part of the Elder Brother
in Milton's *Comus*; he inscribed his copy (which
is now in the Huntington Library, San Marino,
California) with the words (in Latin) 'this book

is most deserving of burning, its author of the gallows'. This judgement, which was typical of English royalist reactions, was echoed in the chancellaries of Europe, and it was to the educated citizens of Europe (especially those of the United Provinces) that Milton addressed his defence of the regicide.

The first response to Milton's tract, *Pro rege et populo Anglicano apologia, contra Johannis Polypragmatici (alias Miltoni Angli) defensionem destructivam regis et populi Anglicani* ('An apology for the king and people of England against the defence, destructive of the king and people of England, by John the Multifarious, alias Milton the Englishman') was a plodding refutation in inept Latin (and subsequently in competent Dutch) published anonymously in Antwerp; it was popularly attributed to John Bramhall, but actually written by John Rowland. Milton decided, possibly for reasons of health, not to respond to this tract; the *Responsio* was instead written by his nephew John Phillips.

Milton had realized before his wife Mary's return in 1645 that he was losing the sight in his left eye, and by 1648 the eye had ceased to function. Early in 1652 his right eye collapsed, and Milton became permanently blind; he could no longer see his son, John, who had been born on 16 March 1651. In the following year, early in May 1652, Mary Milton died shortly after giving birth to their daughter Deborah, and Milton was left, alone and blind, to care for four young children; six weeks later, his only son, John, died. Later that year Milton was evicted from his Whitehall apartment, and on 17 December he moved with his three surviving children into a house in Petty France opening on to St James's Park; he stayed in this house until the Restoration.

In August 1652 an anonymous tract called *Regii sanguinis clamor ad coelum adversus parricidas Anglicanos* ('A cry to heaven of the king's blood against the English parricides') was published in The Hague. The *Clamor* contains a brutal personal attack on Milton in its opening pages, and concludes with a 245-line poem that renews the attack. The author of this work was almost certainly the Anglican divine Peter Du Moulin, who sent it to Salmasius in order that it could be published in the Netherlands; Salmasius passed the manuscript to Alexander More, a minister of the Reformed church. More (Latin Morus) contributed a preface to Du Moulin's treatise, and sent it to Adriaan Vlacq, who published it in The Hague. Milton mistakenly assumed that More was the author of the treatise, and although he was apprised of his error by John Durie and Samuel Hartlib, he stood by his mistake and flatly refused to be dissuaded. In May 1654 Milton replied to the *Clamor* with *Joannis Miltonii Angli pro populo Anglicano defensio secunda, contra infamem libellum anonymum cui titulus 'Regii sanguinis clamor ad coelum adversus parricidas Anglicanos'* ('The second defence of John Milton, Englishman, on behalf of the English people, against an infamous anonymous libel entitled A cry to heaven of the king's blood against the English parricides'). This tract, which is usually known as the *Defensio secunda* or the *Second Defence*, is for two important reasons less republican than its predecessor:

first, Oliver Cromwell had assumed the quasi-regal title lord protector in December 1653, and so Milton praises him in terms that befit a monarch; second, the need to restore relations with Sweden leads Milton to formulate a paean of praise for Queen Kristina.

The *Clamor* alleged that Milton had been expelled from Cambridge and had fled in shame to Italy. Milton decided to combat this calumny by defending himself and attacking More. Milton's self-defence is a long account of his youth in which he presents himself as the epitome of moral probity in Cambridge and as a courageous protestant champion in Italy. His attack on More centres on sexual indiscretions, particularly More's seduction of a servant in the household of Salmasius. Milton seizes on this violation of Christian morality and of the hospitality of his host to pummel More, constantly playing on More's name in Latin and Greek (in which it can mean 'mulberry tree' and 'fool'), and proposing an analogy between an immoral sexual act and an immoral book; in this unnatural coupling of minister and servant,

Milton alleges, both sinners became pregnant: the servant gave birth to a bastard child and the minister of the gospel gave birth to an evil book, the *Clamor*.

In October 1654 the deeply wounded Alexander More hit back at Milton with *Alexandri Mori ecclesiasticae et sacrarum litterarum professoris fides publica, contra calumnias Ioannis Miltoni* ('The public faith of Alexander More, minister and professor of sacred literature, against the misrepresentations of John Milton'); in the following spring he published a *Supplementum* which consists for the most part of additional evidence. These two tracts are largely concerned with personal morality (Milton's is attacked, More's defended) and with Milton's doggedly mistaken insistence that More was the author of the *Clamor*. Milton replied in August 1655 with his third and final defence, *Joannis Miltonii Angli pro se defensio contra Alexander Morum, ecclesiasten, libelli famosi, cui titulus, 'Regii sanguinis clamor'...authorem recte dictum* ('The defence of himself of John Milton, Englishman, against the minister Alexander More, who is rightly said to be the author of a famous libel entitled Cry of the royal blood'), in which Milton defends his own morality, attacks More's, and defends his indefensible attribution of the *Clamor* to More.

## Poetry, 1652–1659

Milton's public voice may have echoed around Europe during the 1650s, but most of the poems that he was writing remained unpublished until 1673. In August 1653 Milton had returned to the Psalms, producing verse translations of psalms 1–8. His other poetical works of the 1650s were all sonnets. The sonnet had hitherto been a form used primarily to express the love of a man for a woman or (in the case of John Donne) for God. Milton chose instead to use the sonnet as a vehicle for principled statements on public affairs. The earliest sonnet from this period is 'To the Lord General Cromwell' (later Sonnet 16), which Milton dated 'May 1652'. Two months later, on 3 July, he composed a sonnet (later Sonnet 17) to Sir Henry

Vane the younger and sent it to him. The next five sonnets seem to have been composed in 1655. The powerful 'On the late massacre in Piedmont' (later Sonnet 18), which articulates Milton's horror at the barbarous massacre of some 1700 Vaudois in April 1655, was probably composed two months later, in the last week of June. The date of 'On his Blindness' (Sonnet 19), a title first used in 1752, is unknown; several strands of evidence point to the second half of 1655, but it could have been written as early as 1651, when Milton was enduring the final stages of encroaching blindness. The sonnet 'Lawrence of virtuous father' (later Sonnet 20) was probably composed late in 1655, as were the two sonnets addressed to Cyriack Skinner (later Sonnets 21 and 22).

On 12 November 1656 Milton married Katherine Woodcock (*bap.* 1628, *d.* 1658) and in the following October Katherine gave birth to a daughter, who was named after her mother. Four months later Katherine died, and a month later their infant daughter was buried beside her. If, as seems likely but not certain, Milton's wife

Katherine is the subject of 'Methought I Saw my
Late Espoused Saint' (later Sonnet 23), Milton
must have composed the poem in the wake of her
death on 3 February 1658. Shortly thereafter he
began to dictate *Paradise Lost*, though he regularly interrupted his work on the epic to attend to
ecclesiastical and political issues in a final flurry of
political tracts, the last of which appeared on the
eve of the Restoration.

## Prose, 1659–1660

One of the debates that had persisted throughout the Commonwealth and protectorate republic
concerned Erastianism. In 1659 Thomas Erastus's
*Explicatio gravissimae quaestionis* (1589) appeared
in English translation as *The Nullity of Church
Censures*, so giving a wide audience to Erastus's
view that in a state with one religion, the juris-
diction of the state should extend to ecclesiastical
as well as civil matters. Milton was resolutely
opposed to Erastianism, and in February 1659
published *A treatise of civil power in ecclesiastical causes, showing that it is not lawful for any*

*power on earth to compel in matters of religion.* Once again the tract is addressed to parliament, this time to the parliament of Richard Cromwell, which had been convened on 27 January. Milton's short book is a polemic directed 'against Erastus and state-tyranny over the church'.

The argument about Erastian principles was closely related to the argument about tithes, which were compulsory ecclesiastical taxes levied by local churches. Radical Independents opposed tithes on theological grounds (they were said to have emerged from the law of the Old Testament rather than the new dispensation heralded by Jesus), but also because tithes were used to support either the state church from which they wished to dissociate themselves or the secular impropriators into whose families had passed the rectorial tithes that had formerly gone to the monasteries. Milton set out his position on tithes in *Considerations touching the likeliest means to remove hirelings out of the church, wherein is also discoursed of tithes, church-fees, church revenues, and whether any maintenance of ministers can be settled by law*, which was published in August 1659. This tract is again addressed to parliament, but to a different parliament: Richard Cromwell had abdicated on 25 May, and the Rump Parliament had re-established the Commonwealth. In this tract Milton praises the Rump as 'the best patrons of religious and civil liberty that ever these islands brought forth', and asks them to deliver England 'from the oppressions of a simonious decimating clergy'. The phrase recalls Milton's denunciation of the 'blind mouths' of the greedy clergy in 'Lycidas'.

On 13 October 1659 General John Lambert dissolved the Rump Parliament, and on 29 October Milton expressed his dismay about this *coup d'état* in *A Letter to a Friend, Concerning the Ruptures of the Commonwealth*. The identity of the friend is not known, but it is clearly a senior political figure, perhaps the dying John Bradshaw, who may have been related to Milton and who bequeathed £10 to Milton when he died a few weeks later. In this letter, first published by John Toland in 1698, Milton explains to his influential friend that he deplores the 'backsliding' action of the army in deposing the parliament that they had recently restored, and waxes indignant that a state army could 'subdue the supreme power that set them up'. In Milton's view, the civil power, be it parliament or council of state, must always be the supreme power.

In the first fortnight of November 1659 Milton dictated *Proposals of certain expedients for the preventing of a civil war now feared, and the settling of a firm government*, a short tract not published until 1938; the surviving text seems to be a draft or a briefing document rather than a completed work. The tone of the pamphlet is much less combative than that of *A Letter to a Friend*; parliament is defended, but the army is not attacked. Milton proposes that England be governed by a 'Grand or Supreme Council' in which members 'sit indissolubly' for the rest of their lives; he rejects the term 'parliament' for this body on the grounds that it is a 'Norman or French word, a monument of our ancient servitude'.

From 18 to 21 February 1660, when the Commonwealth was on the verge of collapse, Milton dictated a passionate pamphlet entitled *The ready and easy way to establishing a free commonwealth, and the excellence thereof compared with the inconveniences and dangers of re-admitting kingship in this nation*, which was published before the end of the month. In the face of a Restoration that looked increasingly inevitable, Milton chose defiantly to set the bondage of monarchy against the freedom of a Christian commonwealth ruled by a grand council. This council would be both permanent and self-perpetuating; Milton was not an instinctive democrat, and did not think that popular elections were an appropriate mechanism for filling vacancies in the council.

Early in March Milton dictated *The present means and brief delineation of a free commonwealth, easy to be put in practice, and without delay*, the manuscript of which has disappeared; when John Toland published it in 1698 he added the words *In a Letter to General Monck*, a reasonable inference from the content of what seems to be the draft of a letter. The formal title, more likely to be Milton's than Toland's, implies that Milton had intended to write a pamphlet in the form of an open letter rather than a private letter to George Monck. The letter summarizes the proposals of *The Ready and Easy Way*, but with two important differences: the authority of the grand council would be limited so that it would not have the 'power to endanger our liberty', and the establishment of the council should be implemented even if there were opposition, if necessary by military force.

Milton soon set to work on the second edition of *The Ready and Easy Way*, revised at the end of March to accommodate the headlong rush of political change in the last days of the English republic; the tract was published in the first week of April, a month before the restoration of Charles II was proclaimed on 8 May. Milton's eloquent defence of the nobility of republican values and his horrific vision of the degeneracy and servitude that would follow in the wake of a restored monarchy make this pamphlet England's greatest monument to a lost political cause.

The government that he proposes is not a direct democracy: Milton opposes 'committing all to the noise and shouting of a rude multitude', a phrase that anticipates the contempt of the Jesus of *Paradise Regained* for the 'miscellaneous rabble'. Instead he envisages an aristocracy of godly men, an ideal that recalls the assumption in *Comus* and *Of Education* that rulers should be an aristocracy of virtue. This argument leads Milton to the conclusion that the enlightened minority should be able to impose liberty on the ignorant majority, if necessary by force.

On 25 March Matthew Griffith, a former chaplain of Charles I, preached a royalist sermon which he published at the beginning of April as *The Fear of God and the King*. Milton replied, probably in the second week of April, with *Brief Notes upon a Late Sermon*—his last publication before the Restoration cut off his access to the medium of print. Milton expresses his satisfaction that the council of state had been quick to incarcerate Griffith, and goes on to denounce him for advocating episcopacy and for dedicating the sermon to Monck. Milton concludes that if England is about to submit to the thraldom of monarchy, it should at least choose its own monarch: Milton thought that Monck would be a better choice than Charles Stuart. Milton's last republican tract thus advocated the second-best choice of an elected monarch. Milton was not a constitutional theorist, but it is in these tracts written in the final years of the interregnum that he articulates a shifting compromise in which he adapts the republican values that he had celebrated for more than a decade to an unstable and uncertain political situation.

One of Milton's private projects during his years as a servant of the Commonwealth and protectorate was the composition of a systematic theology. This ordonnance began as a compilation of theological writings in the 1640s, and was successively described as a 'System of Divinity', a 'Body of Divinity', and *'Idea Theologiae'*. The preparation of this treatise was broken off by the Restoration; it survives as a working document, frozen in time by the cataclysm of the Restoration.

How far the raw materials of the treatise have been assimilated into Milton's own thinking is unclear, and the arrangement of some chapters may not reflect Milton's final judgement. There was an abortive attempt to publish the treatise in the Netherlands shortly after Milton's death, but the manuscript was impounded by the English government, together with a collection of Milton's state papers, and was locked in a cupboard in Whitehall and forgotten until rediscovered in November 1823. By that time (or possibly at that time) the manuscript had acquired the Augustinian title *De doctrina Christiana*, and it was published in Latin and in English translation in 1825.

Milton's theology evolved throughout his adult life, and *De doctrina* and *Paradise Lost* represent his thinking in the 1650s and 1660s. Many of his theological ideas would have been regarded as unsound or even heretical by his contemporaries. He rejected the doctrine of the Trinity in favour of a modified Arianism, insisted on the materiality of angels and denied that the world had been created out of nothing; his understanding of divine grace and of soteriology aligned him with the Arminians rather than the Calvinists, and so the Adam and Eve of *Paradise Lost* exercise free choice.

# Milton's Paradise

## Imprisonment and pardon

The restoration of Charles II was proclaimed on 8 May 1660, and Milton went into hiding at the house of an unidentified friend in Bartholomew Close (West Smithfield). On 16 June an order for Milton's arrest was issued, and on 13 August a proclamation ordering books by Milton to be called in for burning was published; on 27 August copies of his books were duly burnt by the public executioner at the Old Bailey. Milton's life hung in the balance until 29 August, when the Act of Free and General Pardon, Indemnity and Oblivion was given the royal assent; Milton was not named as an exception to the general pardon, so he escaped the death penalty, while none the less remaining liable to arrest and assassination. Milton emerged from hiding and took a house in Holborn (in the parish of St Giles-in-the-Fields), where he lived until the autumn, when he was arrested and imprisoned in the Tower. On 15 December he was ordered to be released from the Tower and to pay the cost of his imprisonment, which was set at £150. Milton had been pardoned, but no copy of the pardon has survived (even though two copies survived long enough to be entered into indexes in the Public Record Office, now the National Archives), so the precise reason for his release is not known. One effect of the Restoration had been the collapse of the Excise Office, which took with it Milton's savings of £2000. He emerged from prison in financial difficulty, and promptly protested against what he saw as the excessive fee for his imprisonment. On 17 December the poet and politician Andrew Marvell raised the matter in parliament, which referred it to the committee of privileges; the eventual outcome is not known. On his release from prison Milton moved to a house on Jewin Street, where he lived until about 1669.

On 24 February 1663 Milton married for the third time. He was fifty-four and his red-haired bride, Elizabeth Minshull (1638–1727), was twenty-four; she outlived her husband by more than half a century. By this stage Milton seems to have been estranged from his daughters: on being informed of her father's impending wedding, Mary replied (according to Milton's servant) 'that it was no news, to hear of his wedding, but, if she could hear of his death, *that* was something' (Masson, 4.476). The visitation of plague in 1665 was unusually virulent, and in July the Miltons moved to a cottage in Chalfont St Giles, a Quaker village in Buckinghamshire. The cottage belonged to Anne Fleetwood, daughter of the regicide George Fleetwood, and had been rented on Milton's behalf by the Quaker Thomas Ellwood; the cottage is the only residence of Milton still standing, and is now a museum. Milton returned to London when the plague had abated, probably in February 1666.

On 2 September 1666 the conflagration later known as the great fire of London began to spread through the city, and three days later two-thirds of London had been consumed. Milton's home in Jewin Street was just north of the city wall, but in the event the fire was successfully contained on its northern flank by the wall and the ditch. Milton's house was safe, but most of his London had disappeared, including his childhood home on Bread Street, his school, and St Paul's Cathedral. In 1670 Milton lodged for a time in Duck Lane, Little Britain. The reason for this temporary accommodation is not known, but it may have been occasioned by the move from Jewin Street to Milton's last home, in Artillery Walk (now Bunhill Row).

## *Paradise Lost*

The Restoration interrupted Milton's composition of *Paradise Lost*, which assumed its final form in the years 1658–63. The remote beginnings of his epic can be seen in four drafts of a tragedy called 'Paradise Lost' (in the third draft) or 'Adam Unparadised' (in the fourth draft) which survive in the Trinity College manuscript; these drafts seem to have been written about 1640. Edward Phillips claimed that he had been shown part of

Satan's first soliloquy (*Paradise Lost*, book 5, ll. 32–41) 'several years before the poem was begun', when Milton still intended it to be a tragedy rather than an epic. The difficulties of composing such a long and complex work were exacerbated by Milton's difficult personal circumstances and by his blindness. He seems to have composed during the winter months, usually at night or in the early morning; when an amanuensis arrived he would dictate the lines that he had composed (usually about forty), and then 'reduce them to half the number'. Edward Phillips would then correct the spelling and punctuation of 'ten, twenty or thirty verses at a time'. Composition of the poem was inevitably interrupted by Milton's months in hiding and in prison, and when he eventually resumed his dictation, his world had changed irrevocably; at the beginning of book 7 the narrator's voice acknowledges that:

> More safe I sing with mortal voice, unchanged
> To hoarse or mute, though fallen on evil days,
> On evil days though fallen, and evil tongues;
> In darkness, and with dangers compassed round,
> And solitude.

This is the voice of a blind poet whose life was in danger after the calamity of the Restoration. Milton had aspired in the opening invocation of the poem 'to justify the ways of God to men', and the collapse of the godly republic had certainly left God's ways in need of justification. Milton's view was that the Commonwealth had failed not because God had caused it to fail, but rather because the frailty of humankind can be successfully exploited by the forces of evil. The Satan whom Milton created in *Paradise Lost* is not a king in exile who conquers Eden by force, but rather a traitor who speaks the language of radical republicanism in order to advance his own interests; in this respect *Paradise Lost* reflects Milton's contention that the reign of the godly was betrayed from within. Despite this reflection of the time of crisis during which the poem was composed, *Paradise Lost* is neither a political allegory nor a *roman-à-clef*; it is rather an epic which aspires to achieve in English what Homer, Virgil, and Dante had achieved in their languages, and its avowed purpose is theological rather than political. He aspired in his epic, as he had many years earlier in *Of Education*, 'to repair the ruins of our first parents by regaining to know God aright'. He saw himself as a latter-day prophet chosen by God to explain the divine ways to those who would know God aright, and he hoped that *Paradise Lost* would 'fit audience find, though few' (book 31); the godly survivors of the republic had the requisite fitness, and it is to them that Milton addressed his poem. The godly government of the interregnum had been displaced by the profligate court of Charles II, and for those who had laboured for the good old cause, God's ways stood in need of justification.

*Paradise Lost* is an epic which accommodates within that genre several other genres: the account of Sin and Death is an allegory, the description of Eden is pastoral, the gardening labours of Adam and Eve are georgic and, most important of all, the fall of Adam and Eve is presented as a tragedy. Milton describes the fall in book 9, at the outset of which he declares that he 'now must change / Those notes to tragic', so signalling that he proposes to transform the crime and punishment narrative of the biblical account of the fall into a tragedy. It is this shift of genre that has necessitated the endowment of Adam and Eve with dramatic characters and with motives for their actions. The sympathetic presentation of these motives, together with the detailed account of the role of Satan in the fall of Eve, constitutes a plea in mitigation for the fall. Milton's version of the fall is thus an affirmation of the dignity of humankind, a sentiment rooted in the Renaissance rather than the Reformation and one which, on a political level, explains to God the human failings that led to the fall of the godly republic. In this respect, Milton was attempting to justify the ways of men to God.

The focus of *Paradise Lost* is the fall of Adam and Eve, but the action is also played out on a cosmic stage in which the principal characters are God, the Son, and Satan. Milton's seventeenth-century God is much more anthropomorphic than his twenty-first century descendant in which Milton's readers believe or disbelieve. The God of *Paradise Lost* can be ill-tempered and irrational, and to a modern reader can seem shockingly immodest in his insistence that the purpose of creation is to praise him. Milton's Son is also rooted in the century in which he was conceived. He does not have a pre-incarnate name, and is simply called the Son: in *Paradise Regained* Milton was to deploy his earthly name of Jesus, but he never used the term Christ to denote his character; indeed, he eschewed the term in all poems after 1646, when he used it in 'On the new forcers of conscience'. Milton's Son, like his New Testament original, 'came not to send peace, but a sword' and in *Paradise Lost*, he is, like the angels, primarily a warrior. The accounts of the war in heaven in book 6 and of the creation in book 7 both culminate in a celebration of the Son, whose achievements occlude the work of God the Father. In Puritan soteriology it was the Son rather than the Father who effected salvation, and so the Son is the central figure in the puritan godhead.

In the minds of many of its readers, the most important character in *Paradise Lost* is Milton's Satan, who dominates the first two books of the poem and in a magnificent soliloquy at the beginning of book 4 tries to establish himself as a tragic figure. Seventeenth-century readers shared with Milton an unshakeable conviction of the total and irredeemable depravity of Satan and so regarded him as a falsely heroic figure, but in succeeding centuries, as Enlightenment ideas eroded Christian belief, Satan gradually came to be seen as the truly heroic figure at the imaginative heart of the poem. In the nineteenth century Romantic Satanism spread through Germany as far as Russia, and in the twentieth century Milton was often said to have had an unconscious sympathy with the Satan of *Paradise Lost*.

*Paradise Lost* was finally completed by 1663, but Milton's reputation as a champion of the republic meant that he could not publish the poem immediately. The politically opportune moment for the publication of *Paradise Lost* finally arose in the spring of 1667. On 27 April Milton sealed a contract (now in the British Library) with the printer Samuel Simmons; Milton received £5 immediately, with the promise of another £5 when the first edition of 1300 copies had been sold; the second and third editions, neither of which would exceed 1500 copies, would each generate an additional £5. Had the poem proved to be particularly popular, Milton stood to make £20. The first edition was exhausted in the spring of 1669, and on 26 April Simmons paid Milton another £5; the price seems to have been 3*s*. a copy, and so Simmons would have received £195. Milton died shortly after the second edition was published, and so he received only £10 for *Paradise Lost*; after his death his widow sold the rights to the poem to Simmons for £8. The sums involved are modest but quite normal, and certainly no more derisory than the royalties paid by publishers in succeeding centuries.

Milton's epic was registered as 'Paradise Lost: a Poem in Ten Books' on 20 August 1667, and was published late in October or early in November. Sir John Denham is said (by Jonathan Richardson the elder) to have come into the House of Commons (which had reconvened on 10 October) carrying a sheet of *Paradise Lost* 'wet from the press' and proclaiming it 'part of the noblest poem that ever was wrote in any language or any age' (Masson, 6.628); by mid-November the poem was the subject of correspondence between John Beale and John Evelyn. The poem did not sell particularly quickly: between 1667 and 1669 six successive title-pages, each for a different issue, were required to sell the first edition of 1300 copies. The first three editions of *Paradise Lost* sold in modest numbers, but the fourth edition, a sumptuous gilt-edged folio published in 1688, was bought by subscription by many of the most influential readers in England, and thereafter the poem came to be widely regarded as England's national epic.

### *Paradise Regained* and *Samson Agonistes*

In August 1665 Milton had shown the unpublished manuscript of *Paradise Lost* to Thomas Ellwood, who read it and told Milton that 'thou hast said much here of *Paradise Lost*, but what hast thou to say of *Paradise Found?*' (Masson, 6.496). In the following year Ellwood visited Milton in

London, and Milton showed him the manuscript
of *Paradise Regained*, graciously telling Ellwood
that 'this is owing to you; for you put it into
my head by the question you put to me at Chalfont' (ibid., 6.654). It is possible that *Paradise
Regained*, which depicts the temptations of Jesus
in the desert, owes its pacific tone to the influence
of the values of the Quaker community at Chalfont St Giles. The Jesus of *Paradise Regained* is
not a warrior like the Son in book 6 of *Paradise
Lost*, but rather a man who outwits his opponent.
Milton's fictional Jesus is not, however, a senti-
mentalized figure: he denounces ordinary citizens
as 'a herd confused, a miscellaneous rabble', so
reflecting Milton's disdain for popular democracy,
and he denounces the cultural accomplishments of
ancient Greece, so reflecting the opinion of Milton
in his late years that worldly learning was a vain
pursuit; in taking this position he approaches the
radical view that education, like riches, constituted an impediment to salvation.

In the autumn of 1671 Milton published *Paradise Regained, a Poem in IV Books, to which is*

*Added Samson Agonistes.* The date of *Paradise Regained* can be ascertained by the testimony of Thomas Ellwood, but there can be no certainty about the date of *Samson Agonistes*. Topical references and stylistic markers show that *Samson* is substantially a post-Restoration work, though scholars debate whether it was written immediately after the Restoration or shortly before publication; on the other hand, echoes of the divorce tracts of the 1640s make an early stage of composition distinctly possible. It is difficult to gainsay the authoritative opinion of Edward Phillips, who noted that its date of composition 'cannot certainly be concluded'; as Henry Todd pointed out in his edition of 1801, *Samson Agonistes* 'furnishes some internal proofs of its having been composed at different periods'.

*Samson Agonistes* is a closet drama intended to be read rather than performed; it is therefore a literary rather than a dramatic work, and so claimed affinity with the plays of classical antiquity, which in seventeenth-century England were read rather than performed. The structure of the play is modelled on that of ancient Greek drama, but the characterization of Samson is resolutely modern. Like Racine, who was at the height of his powers when Milton published *Samson Agonistes*, Milton created a protagonist who was much more self-conscious than were the dramatic characters of antiquity; in this respect Milton's Samson has more in common with Hamlet than with Oedipus. Indeed, Samson is in some respects a Restoration nonconformist struggling to discern a pattern of divine intervention in his life. God is absent from *Samson Agonistes*, as he is in similar works such as John Bunyan's *Pilgrim's Progress*: for late seventeenth-century nonconformists, spiritual growth was not assisted by any vision of God. Samson's massacre of the Philistines at the end of the play also has a contemporary agenda: in Milton's version of the massacre it is only the Philistian lords that are killed, because 'the vulgar only scaped who stood without'. In Milton's view, retribution should be directed at political leaders rather than at those whom they lead.

# 'England hath need of thee'

## Last works and death

In 1669 Milton published his *Accidence commenced grammar, supplied with sufficient rules for the use of such (younger or elder) as are desirous without more trouble than need to attain the Latin tongue, the elder sort especially, with little teaching and their own industry*; it is not clear when Milton had written this primer of Latin accidence (that is, the variable forms of words) and grammar, but it is possible that it was a product of his years as a teacher in the 1640s.

Two years later Milton published his *History of Britain*. The first four books had been drafted in February and March 1649, and the last two books seem to have been written in the mid-1650s, possibly in 1655. The most problematical element in the *History* is the digression, a passage in book 3 which was omitted from all editions until 1738, but published separately in 1681 as *Character of the Long Parliament*; this comparison of the ancient Britons at the time of the Roman withdrawal with the English in Milton's own time was probably written in 1648, but a case for composition in 1660 has been advanced.

In May 1672 Milton published his *Joannis Milton Angli artis logicae plenior institutio ad Petri Rami methodum concinnata, adjucta est praxis analytica & Petri Rami vita* ('A fuller course in the art of logic, arranged according to the method of Pierre de la Ramée; an analytical exercise and a life of La Ramée are appended'). The *Ars logicae* is a derivative Ramist treatise on logic drawn for the most part from a Latin commentary on Petrus Ramus by George Downham, as is the analytical exercise; the biography is a condensed version of the life of Ramus by Johann Freige. In the following year Milton published a revised edition of his minor poems and his first polemical tract since the Restoration, *Of true religion, heresy, schism, toleration and what best means may be used against the growth of popery*, which appeared early in May 1673. Charles II had promulgated the declaration of indulgence (which had suspended the penalties for Catholicism and nonconformity) in March 1672, but had been forced to rescind it in March 1673. Milton's tract is tolerant of the sectarians, who 'may have some errors, but are not heretics', but mounts a coruscating attack on Roman Catholicism, which he denounces as politically dangerous and theologically idolatrous.

In 1674 Milton published a volume containing a collection of thirty-one private letters (*Epistolae familiares*) and the Latin prolusions that he had delivered while a student in Cambridge. He had also saved many of his state papers, most of which were his translations into Latin of letters from the English government to the chancellaries of Europe, but these were not published until after his death. The first edition, *Literae pseudo-senatûs Anglicani Cromwellii reliquorumque perduellium nomine ac jussu conscriptae a Joanne Miltono* ('Letters written by John Milton in the name and by the order of the so-called English parliament of Cromwell and other traitors'), was printed by two different printers (in Amsterdam and Brussels) in October 1676; a preface carefully distances the edition from the politics of the reviled interregnum government by insisting disingenuously that the sole interest of the letters lies in their exemplary Latin style.

Milton's final political work was a translation of the Latin version of *A Declaration, or, Letters Patent*, a Polish tract advocating an elective monarchy; this pamphlet was a contribution to the Exclusion debate, in that it contests the Catholic succession, but its advocacy of a form of monarchy also implies that Milton may not have espoused unequivocally the republicanism with which he came to be associated after his death.

Milton's final publication, early in July 1674, was the second edition of *Paradise Lost*, which he had reorganized into twelve books, so making explicit the parallel with the epics of classical antiquity; this edition also contained two prefatory poems, one in Latin by 'S. B.' (probably Milton's physician friend Samuel Barrow) and one in English by Andrew Marvell. A few weeks after the publication of this edition, Milton prepared a nuncupative (that is, orally declared) will with the help of his brother Christopher. In his will Milton chose to recall with smouldering resentment that his first father-in-law, Richard Powell, had never paid the dowry of £1000 that was due to Milton on his marriage to Mary Powell. According to Christopher's testimony on 23 November, the will stated that 'the portion due to me from Mr Powell, my former wife's father, I leave to the unkind children I had by her, having received no part of it'. This worthless legacy of an unpaid dowry testifies to the bitterness of Milton's estrangement from his daughters; he left everything to Elizabeth, 'my loving wife'. Milton died, probably of renal failure associated with gout, on the night of 9–10 November 1674, at his home in Artillery Walk, and was buried beside his father near the altar in St Giles Cripplegate on 12 November.

**Eighteenth-century Milton: republican and poet**

After his death Milton became associated with the whig cause. His enthusiastic praise of Queen Kristina was forgotten, as was his insistence in the *Defensio secunda* that he had written not against kings, but only against tyrants; instead, Milton came to be regarded as an unambiguous republican. Milton's republican ideas and ideals were eventually taken up in France and America. An anonymous pamphlet called *Théorie de la royauté, d'après la doctrine de Milton* (Paris, 1789) appropriated him to the revolutionary cause in France, and in 1792 Jacobin regicides reissued the French translation of Milton's *Defensio prima*. In the United States, Benjamin Franklin, Thomas Jefferson, and John Adams drew on their wide reading in Milton's poetry and prose to articulate their republicanism: Franklin evoked the Chaos of *Paradise Lost* in his diatribe against British taxes in America, Jefferson deployed the arguments of Milton's anti-prelatical tracts to support the case for ecclesiastical disestablishment in Virginia, and Adams excoriated British rulers as embodiments of the arrogance and futile rebellion of Milton's Satan. Milton may rightly be regarded as one of the founding fathers of American and French republicanism, but in England he had no political progeny; English republicanism died on the scaffold with Algernon Sidney in 1683, and has never been successfully revived.

The 1695 edition of *Paradise Lost* included learned annotations by 'P. H.' (probably Patrick Hume), and so Milton's epic became the first English poem to be edited as if it were a classical text. Thereafter the poem attracted serious critical attention. In 1712 Joseph Addison published a series of 'Notes' on *Paradise Lost* in *The Spectator*, and these notes were soon translated into French (1727), German (1740), and Italian (1742). In 1732 Richard Bentley published an emended edition of *Paradise Lost* in which he 'corrected' hundreds of imagined errors in what he thought was a corrupt text; Bentley's misconceived erudition was soon discredited by scholars and mocked by satirists (including Alexander Pope, who included him in his *Dunciad*), but his edition and the analyses of his detractors demonstrate the care with which educated eighteenth-century readers attended to the text of Milton's poem. Later in the century Samuel Johnson included an insightful and opinionated critical biography of Milton in his *Lives of the Poets* (1779–81).

*Paradise Lost* was written in blank verse, but in the late seventeenth century portions of the poem were twice published in rhymed versions: John Dryden secured the permission of Milton to 'tag' (that is, rhyme) *Paradise Lost* for his operatic adaptation, *The State of Innocence and Fall of Man* (1677), and John Hopkins gallantly tried to offer assistance to ladies who found the poem too difficult by publishing a rhymed paraphrase of books 4 and 9 (1699). During this period translations into German (1682) and Latin (1686) rendered the poem accessible to European audiences.

In the eighteenth century Milton's epic was responsible for the shift from rhyme to blank verse, and also for many features of poetic diction and syntax. The style of *Paradise Lost* was imitated by classical translators such as Pope and Joseph Trapp and by poets including Sir Richard Blackmore, John Dennis, Matthew Smith, and William Thompson; it was also parodied, most notably by John Philips (*The Splendid Shilling*, 1701) and John Gay (*Wine*, 1709). The taste for the picturesque that became an important factor in the gardens, paintings, and nature poetry of the eighteenth century took as its starting point Milton's Eden, a 'happy rural seat of various view'. What was perceived as the awesome seriousness of *Paradise Lost* became the corner-stone of the sublime, a concept so all-pervasive that Mary Wollstonecraft could complain in 1787 that she was 'sick of hearing of the sublimity of Milton'; this was not a complaint about Milton, but rather a protest about the invoking of the sublime as a substitute for a proper critical understanding of Milton's poetry. The process of translation continued apace throughout the eighteenth century, including versions of *Paradise Lost* in Dutch (1728), French (1729), Italian (1729), Greek (1735), Russian (1777), Norwegian

(1787), Portuguese (1791), Polish (1791), Hungarian (1796), and Manx (1796).

## A national and international poet

The appropriation of Milton by the Romantic poets included both critical comment—Percy Bysshe Shelley and William Blake championed Milton's Satan—and creative imitation, most notably *The Prelude*, in which William Wordsworth aspires to establish himself as the successor to Milton. Blake illustrated all of Milton's major poems (except *Samson Agonistes*) and wrote two Miltonic poems, *The Four Zoas* (a rewriting of *Paradise Lost*) and *Milton, a Poem in Two Books*. The political Milton was also taken up as an early radical: as Wordsworth ringingly proclaims in 'London, 1802':

> Milton! thou should'st be living at this hour:
> England hath need of thee.

In the course of the nineteenth century this idolatry led to Milton's enthronement as the national poet; the greatest monument to the national reverence for Milton was David Masson's vast seven-volume biography of the poet. At the same time the tide of faith in Milton's anthropomorphic God and his historical Adam and Eve was beginning to retreat, and the study of Milton seemed to some to be an exhausted endeavour; the literary scholar Sir Walter Raleigh memorably formulated this position when he conceded that '*Paradise Lost* is a monument to dead ideas' (W. Raleigh, *Milton*, 1922, 88). Throughout the century new translations of Milton's poems continued to be published, including versions of *Paradise Lost* in Czech (1811), Spanish (1812), Swedish (1815), Icelandic (1818), Armenian (1819), Welsh (1819), Hebrew (1871), and Tongan (1892).

In the early twentieth century Milton fell 'on evil days and evil tongues' in his native England. The bitterest of those tongues was that of the literary critic F. R. Leavis, who complacently announced in 1933 that 'Milton's dislodgement, in the past decade, after two centuries of predominance, was effected with remarkably little fuss'. This dislodgement, which Leavis attributed to the strictures of T. S. Eliot and J. Middleton Murry, proved to be an illusion beyond the narrow confines of the Cambridge of Leavis's day, though the popular idea of Milton as a grim misogynist has persisted; the most influential embodiment of this image is Robert Graves's *Wife to Mr Milton* (1943).

In the early twenty-first century Milton continues to be widely read. Schoolchildren in many countries still study Milton's poems (especially the sonnet on his blindness), *Paradise Lost* is studied in universities, and there is a substantial scholarly industry devoted to the study of Milton's works. There are large Milton societies in America and in Japan, and the learned presses continue to issue huge numbers of books and articles on Milton; there are even two journals wholly given over to Milton, *Milton Quarterly* and *Milton Studies*. For literary scholars and educated general readers alike, the poetry of Milton retains a central place in the canon of English literature. *Paradise Lost* is widely and rightly regarded as the supreme poetic achievement in the English language, fit to sit alongside the poems of Homer, Virgil, and Dante. In America, where Christianity is still a vital force, *Paradise Lost* is valued as the supreme epic of Christendom. In post-Christian Europe and in secular American circles, *Paradise Lost* has become a cultural battlefield for feminists and Freudians, cultural materialists and new historicists. These ephemeral ideologies have replaced earlier concerns with humanistic values and Christian ideas, and will in turn be supplanted by new critical fashions, but *Paradise Lost* will retain its importance as one of the greatest works of the human imagination.

# *Sources*

D. Masson, *The life of John Milton*, 7 vols. (1859–94) · W. R. Parker, *Milton: a biography*, 2nd edn, ed. G. Campbell, 2 vols. (1996) · J. M. French, *The life records of John Milton*, 5 vols. (1949–58) · G. Campbell, *A Milton chronology* (1997) · J. Shawcross, *Milton: a bibliography for the years 1624–1700* (1984); *Addenda and corrigenda* (1990) · P. Beal, 'Milton', *Index of English literary manuscripts*, ed. P. J. Croft and others, 2/2 (1993), 69–104 · *The works of John Milton*, ed. F. A. Patterson, 18 vols. (1931–8) · H. Darbishire, ed., *The early lives of Milton* (1932) · A. Stern, *Milton und seine Zeit*, 4 vols. in 2 (Leipzig, 1877–9) · D. L. Clark, *Milton at St Paul's School* (1948) · M. Di Cesare, ed., *Milton in Italy* (1991) · C. Hill, *Milton and the English revolution* (1977) · R. Fallon, *Milton in government* (1993) · B. Lewalski, *The life of John Milton*, rev. edn (2003)

# *Index*

## Enjoy biography? Explore more than 55,000 life stories in the Oxford Dictionary of National Biography

The biographies in the 'Very Interesting People' series derive from the *Oxford Dictionary of National Biography*—available in 60 print volumes and online.

To find out about the lives of more than 55,000 people who shaped all aspects of Britain's past worldwide, visit the *Oxford DNB* website at **www.oxforddnb.com**.

### There's lots to discover ...

Read about remarkable people in all walks of life—not just the great and good, but those who left a mark, be they good, bad, or bizarre.

Browse through more than 10,000 portrait illustrations— the largest selection of national portraiture ever published.

Regular features on history in the news—with links to biographies—provide fascinating insights into topical events.

### Get a life ... by email

Why not sign up to receive the free *Oxford DNB* 'Life of the Day' by email? Entertaining, informative, and topical biographies delivered direct to your inbox—a great way to start the day.

### Find out more at www.oxforddnb.com

*'An intellectual wonderland for all scholars and enthusiasts'*

Tristram Hunt, *The Times*